5-Ingredient Cast Iron Skillet Recipes

Louise Davidson

This book is presented solely for motivational and informational purposes. The author and the publisher do not hold any responsibility for errors, omissions, or contrary interpretation of the subject matter herein. The recipes provided in this book are for informational purposes only and are not intended to provide dietary advice. A medical practitioner should be consulted before making any changes in diet. Additionally, recipes' cooking times may require adjustment depending on age and quality of appliances. Readers are strongly urged to take all precautions to ensure ingredients are fully cooked in order to avoid the dangers of foodborne illnesses.

ISBN: 9781704765587

Printed in the United States

www.thecookbookpublisher.com

CONTENTS

INTRODUCTION

Cooking with fewer ingredients is not just a modern *trend*; it has somehow become a modern *necessity* for people who still want to prepare healthy home-cooked meals. After all, nobody wants to come home after a tiring day and have to assemble endless ingredients before they even start cooking. Nobody wants to deal with time-consuming meals that take an entire evening to make. It's a real mood killer.

We're a generation of hardcore minimalists, in all cultures, across the continents. Of course, we all still make elaborate traditional recipes (meals, desserts, snacks, appetizers) for festive events, family get-togethers, holidays and other gatherings. Those celebrations call for serving our families and guests something special. However, in our routine daily lives, we all have to adopt a practical approach that gives us the time to complete the day without any rush or hassle.

5-ingredient cooking is a popular technique with millions of working couples and homemakers. It simplifies your life like anything! These smart recipes use smart combinations of ingredients to provide delicious meals that are quick and easy to make. And with fewer ingredients to use, there are fewer things to get wrong, so you'll never worry about compromising taste or texture.

Of course, we all have some basic cooking ingredients that we keep stored in our pantry, such as cooking oil, butter, black pepper and salt. These ingredients, along with cooking liquids (water, broth, stock etc.) aren't counted against the 5-ingredient limit since you don't have to make a special trip to the store to get them.

And you don't necessarily need to make a special trip for the other ingredients, either. 5-ingredient cooking also makes it easy to make a meal plan in advance and store enough ingredients in the pantry for a whole week or month. Just make a list of the ingredients needed for your favorite recipes and buy them in one go from a supermarket or grocery store.

This cookbook provides an exclusive collection of healthy cast-iron skillet recipes with just 5 ingredients. Explore a wide range of cast-iron recipes for your various cooking needs, including chicken, turkey, pork, beef, lamb, veal, seafood, fish, vegetarian mains and your favorite sides. The recipes are all easy to follow and suitable for both beginners as well as kitchen experts.

Before starting with the recipes, lets get to know the mighty cast iron skillet!

COOKING WITH
CAST IRON COOKWARE

This book was created to show you a more modern approach to using cast iron in your daily cooking. While cast iron has a reputation for rustic campsite cooking, we would be doing it a great disservice by overlooking the sophistication and simplicity that it can bring to your kitchen, every day. If you have been looking for a way to streamline meal preparation, without needing to sacrifice any culinary elements, then you will find great joy in cooking as you embrace the cast iron lifestyle.

Each recipe in this cookbook maximize flavor while reducing effort. With only 5-ingredient, you will be able to whip up delicious meals that can be prepared in just one skillet that can be used on the stove top, in the oven and, in some cases, both. From comfort stews to delicate seafood dishes, your entire meal is contained in one skillet that has enhanced both the flavor and character of your favorite dishes.

This chapter will cover everything you need to know about getting your cast iron skillet ready and keeping it perfect condition as cast iron cookware last forever.

Brief History of Cast Iron

While we often think of cast iron as something fairly new, it has actually been around since the 5th century BC. In fact, cast iron artefacts have been discovered from Ancient China, where it is believed to have been invented.

Originally used to make ploughshares, the Ancient Chinese also used it to make pots and even weapons. However, despite how old cast iron is, it did not come to Europe until the 15th century AD. During this time, cast iron was used for cannons.

In the 1700's, a man by the name of Abraham Darby began creating pots and kettles from cast iron when he found a way to produce the pots with a thinner amount of iron. It was through this process that owning cast iron became a popular choice in the 18th and 19th century and cast iron cookware has been found in homes ever since, even passed down from one generation to the next.

It was introduce to America thanks to settlers who brought along during their transatlantic journey.

Nowadays cast irons have regain popularity after a decline during the 20th century because of the health benefits of cooking with cast iron and the fact that other material use for cookware may presents some health concerns.

Cast Iron Cooking Tips

There are a few things to know about cast iron cooking, which we will detail in just a bit. However, first there are a few tricks that will help make your one skillet cooking even easier, and reducing the time you spend in the kitchen.

- First, know your recipe and have all of your ingredients ready. Because cast iron holds heat so effectively, you may find that food cooks a little faster than you are accustomed to. Where before you might have time to leisurely chop ingredients while you are cooking, you might find that when using cast iron, it works better to have everything prepared beforehand.

- Take advantage of preparing ingredients ahead of time. An easy cast iron skillet dinner can be put together with any number of fresh produce and meats with the addition of precooked pasta or grains, most of which can be conveniently stored in your freezer until ready to use. When it comes to pastas, many times the noodles can cooked directly in the skillet with the use of a few cups of broth or water. However, it is also good to have some precooked noodles available, lightly dressed in olive oil to prevent sticking. These are perfect for dishes with cream based sauces.

- Experiment often. As you begin to create the recipes in this book, take notice of preparation techniques and the general style of foods presented and begin to experiment on your own. The more you do this the more comfortable you will become with using cast iron.

- You do not need an entire cast iron set. Don't think that you need to invest in an entire set of cookery that you feel you will barely use. Instead, choose one large skillet. The recipes in this book are all prepared in either a 10-inch or 12-inch skillet. You can reduce the recipes and use smaller skillets for many of these recipes as well, however if you only have one piece of cast iron, a larger skillet will provide greater versatility.

Care and Use of Cast Iron Skillets

Caring for and using your cast iron skillet requires just a few special accommodations, but that doesn't mean it is more difficult or troublesome to use than any other type of cookware. Following is some advice on how to get the most out of using your cast iron cookware.

Seasoning

To begin with, your cast iron needs a good seasoning, and we are not talking about spice. The act of seasoning your cast iron skillet is the processes of applying thin layers of oil and heating it repeatedly. What this does is break down the cooking oil into a type of polymerized oil. More simply put, seasoning your pan creates a barrier between your food and the pan, making it non-stick, increasing its lifespan, and reducing the possibility of the metal interacting with more acidic ingredients. Your pan will need to be seasoned when you first purchase it, and then periodically throughout its life. There are two different methods of seasoning your cast iron skillet:

Method 1

1. Preheat the oven to 350°F.

2. Wash the new skillet. This can be done with warm, soapy water, and a sponge. Do not use steel wool as you can scratch the pan and ruin it. Wash it thoroughly. It should be noted that this is the only time you use soapy water

when cleaning the cast iron. After it is seasoned, do not use soap.

3. Rinse the skillet, and make sure that it is completely free of soap.

4. Dip a paper towel in vegetable oil.

5. Rub the oiled paper towel over the cast iron skillet. You should cover both the inside and outside of the cast iron skillet. Make sure it is a thick, even coat on the skillet.

6. Place in the preheated oven. Make sure the skillet is upside down and in the center of the oven.   To catch oil drips, put a baking sheet or aluminum foil under it.

7. Bake the cast iron skillet for an hour. Do not remove it sooner than an hour or the seasoning process won't be perfect.

8. Turn off the oven but leave the cast iron skillet in the oven.

9. Allow it to cool completely. Cast iron holds heat for a long time so it may take several hours to cool.

10. Wipe away any excess oil if necessary. You do not want to wipe all of the oil off. You want a smooth, shiny skillet but you don't want puddles of oil in your pan.

And that is all you need to do. Repeat whenever your skillet looks rusted or dull. General cooking, especially when using oil, will often keep the pan seasoned.

Method 2

1. Take your cast iron skillet and pour in a layer of coarse salt thick enough to cover the entire bottom without being able to see through it. Add enough cooking oil to cover the salt.

2. Heat the oil over medium heat until it begins to produce smoke. (Increase the temperature if necessary.)

3. Carefully pour off the salt and oil mixture into a heat-proof container and set aside until cooled down completely and discard.
4. Using a clean, soft cloth, buff the inside of the pan until it is smooth.

Cleaning

While you may hear some people say that cast iron doesn't need to be cleaned after every use, the truth is that is does, just in a manner different from what you may be used to. Contrary to popular belief, water is not the nemesis of cast iron, especially a pan that has been properly seasoned. After each use, rinse out your pan, using a very mild soap only if necessary and dry thoroughly. The important point here is the drying. If you leave any moisture in the pan before you put it away it may rust. From time to time you may have bits of food caked onto your skillet that cannot be easily removed. Resist the temptation to use abrasive scouring materials, as these will damage the oil coating of your seasoning and eventually the pan itself. Instead use a salt and fat method similar to the seasoning mentioned above, except with lesser quantities and lower heat. Use a cloth to gently loosen stuck food, with the salt acting as an abrasive and the fat acting as a lubricant.

Re-seasoning

After each use make sure that the skillet is dried thoroughly. You might find that placing a freshly rinsed skillet on a burner over high heat will help evaporate any moisture left behind. Using a paper towel, rub a small amount of cooking oil over the surface and heat until it smokes. Remove it from the heat and let it cool. Over time your seasoning layer will be built up to the point that this becomes something that only needs to be done occasionally.

Preparing to Cook

Cast iron is great because it retains heat very efficiently — it gets hot and it stays hot. However, the thermal conductivity of cast iron is a little lower, which means a cast iron skillet is prone to hot spots, or areas where food may cook faster than others. You might find this beneficial for some dishes, however, for the most part you are going to want to prepare your skillet by placing it dry over a heat source for several minutes before you begin cooking, to minimize this effect. Rotate the skillet every 30 seconds or so, to help spread the heat evenly throughout the pan.

Acidity

The metal in your cast iron skillet may react with certain acidic foods and alter the taste as well as deteriorate your skillet. It isn't necessary to avoid acidic foods altogether; however it is important to keep your pan properly seasoned when working with acidic foods and to limit the time acidic foods are in the pan whenever possible. For example, tomatoes and tomato sauces are added as complements to dishes with no problems. However, it isn't advised to make a tomato sauce from scratch, requiring hours of simmering, in a cast iron pan. Deglazing with wine is delicious and acceptable as long as the deglazing process is kept to just a couple of minutes.

Savory and Sweet

Cast iron tends to hold on to some flavors. For this reason, if you plan on doing a lot of cast iron cooking, invest in at least two separate pieces; one for sweet and one for savory dishes. This will prevent your apple crisp from having a hint of seared steak with mushrooms!

There you have the basics of cast iron cooking. It really isn't intimidating at all. Next, all you need to do is tackle the recipes that follow and enjoy.

BREAKFASTS

Spicy Breakfast Scramble

Serves 6 | Prep. time 5 minutes | Cooking time 10 minutes

Ingredients:
12 eggs
1 red onion
1 jalapeno
2 tablespoons of chives, diced
2 tablespoons of butter, unsalted
1/4 teaspoon of salt
1/4 teaspoon of black pepper
1/2 cup of goat cheese (1/2 cup of feta cheese or cheddar cheese as a substitute for goat cheese)

Directions
1. Place a large, 12" cast iron skillet on the stove, and set the heat to medium.
2. Wash, peel, and dice the red onion.
3. Wash and cut the jalapeno into circles. Keep the seeds with the cut pepper.
4. Add the butter to the skillet and melt.
5. Pour in the onion and jalapeno, and sauté for about 5 to 7 minutes or until the peppers and onions are soft.
6. In a separate bowl, whisk together the eggs.
7. Whisk in the salt and pepper.
8. Pour the eggs into the skillet and cook, stirring frequently, until you have the desired consistency. Usually takes about 3 to 5 minutes.

9. While the eggs are cooking, crumble the goat cheese. If you are using cheddar cheese, shred it, or crumble the feta cheese.
10. Wash and dice the fresh chives.

Nutrition (per serving)
Calories 218, fat 15.3 g, carbs 4 g, protein 17 g, sodium 656 mg

Farm House Breakfast

Serves 4 | Prep. time 20 minutes | Cooking time 30 minutes

Ingredients:
3 cups of red skinned potatoes
8 eggs
1/4 cup of parsley leaves, chopped and fresh
1/4 teaspoon of black pepper
3 tablespoons of butter
1 teaspoon of salt
2 garlic cloves
1 cup of farmhouse cheddar, shredded

Directions
1. Preheat the oven to 400°F.
2. Wash the potatoes, but do not peel them.
3. Chop the potatoes into small hash browns, usually smaller than a half inch.
4. Wash and chop the parsley leaves.
5. Place a 10" to 12" cast iron skillet onto the stove, and set the heat to medium.
6. Add the butter, and allow the butter to melt completely.
7. Place the potatoes into the butter, and sauté for about 15 minutes or until the potatoes are tender and have started to brown.
8. Mince the garlic, and stir into the potatoes, cook for an additional minute.
9. Fold in the salt and pepper.
10. Add the parsley, cook for another minute.
11. Remove the cast iron pan from the stove.
12. Using the back of a wooden spoon, create an indent into the potato. Make 4 indents; one for two eggs.
13. Carefully break two eggs into each indentation.

14. Place in the oven, and bake until the egg whites are cooked. This usually takes about 10 minutes.
15. Once the eggs have the consistency you want, shred the farmhouse cheese.
16. Remove the cast iron skillet from the oven and sprinkle the cheese over the eggs.
17. Return to the oven, and bake for 1 to 2 minutes or until the cheese has melted.
18. Remove from the oven and serve warm.

Nutrition (per serving)
Calories 223, fat 10.8 g, carbs 12 g, protein 19 g, sodium 689 mg

APPETIZERS AND SIDES

Mustard Beer Shrimp Appetizer

Serves 4 | Prep. time 5–10 minutes | Cooking time 8–10 minutes

Ingredients
1 cup whole-wheat pastry flour or all-purpose flour
1 cup light-colored beer (such as pale ale)
½ teaspoon salt (divided)
2 tablespoons canola oil
1 teaspoon Dijon mustard
1 pound raw shrimp with tails, peeled and deveined
Ground black pepper to taste

Directions
1. In a medium-large mixing bowl, combine the mustard, beer, flour and ¼ teaspoon of the salt.
2. Whisk to mix well.
3. Add the oil to a cast-iron skillet and heat it over medium-high heat.
4. One by one, pick the shrimp up by their tails and coat evenly with the batter.
5. Add the shrimp to the skillet one by one and stir-cook for 3–4 minutes until evenly golden. You may need to cook them in two batches.
6. Transfer the shrimp to a serving plate and season with the black pepper and remaining salt.
7. Serve warm.

Nutrition (per serving)
Calories 173, fat 7 g, carbs 7 g, protein 16 g, sodium 825 mg

Bean Stuffed Peppers

*Serves/Yield 32 halved peppers | Prep. time 10–15 minutes |
Cooking time 2 minutes*

Ingredients
¼ cup fresh cilantro leaves, plus more to garnish
3 tablespoons apple cider vinegar
3 tablespoons water
1 teaspoon cumin seeds
1 (15-ounce) can garbanzos/chickpeas, rinsed and drained
16 miniature sweet peppers, halved lengthwise
¼ teaspoon salt

Directions
1. Add the cumin seeds to a cast-iron skillet and toast them, while stirring, over medium-high heat for 1–2 minutes until aromatic.
2. Add the cumin seeds and the other ingredients except for the peppers to a food processor or blender. Blend to make a smooth mixture.
3. Stuff the peppers with the prepared mixture; add some more cilantro on top, if desired.
4. Refrigerate and serve or serve right away.

Nutrition (per pepper half)
Calories 15, fat 0 g, carbs 3 g, protein 1 g, sodium 36 mg

Bacon Stuffed Tomatoes

Serves 3–4 | Prep. time 5–10 minutes
Cooking time 10–12 minutes

Ingredients
2 tablespoons cream cheese
1 tablespoon milk
½ cup blue cheese, crumbled
3 cooked bacon slices, crumbled
1 pint cherry tomatoes

Directions
1. Arrange the bacon slices in a cast-iron skillet, leaving some space between them.
2. Cook over medium heat for 10–12 minutes until crisp.
3. Let cool and drain over paper towels, then crumble.
4. Hollow out the tomatoes to create space for stuffing.
5. Add the cream cheese, blue cheese, milk and bacon to a mixing bowl. Combine well.
6. Stuff the cheese mixture into the cherry tomatoes and serve fresh.

Nutrition (per serving)
Calories 132, fat 10 g, carbs 4 g, protein 7 g, sodium 384 mg

Garlic Shrimp Appetizer

*Serves 10–12 | Prep. time 5–10 minutes |
Cooking time 2 minutes*

Ingredients
¼ cup lemon juice
¼ cup fresh parsley, minced
3 tablespoons minced garlic
2 tablespoons extra-virgin olive oil
½ teaspoon ground black pepper
½ teaspoon kosher salt
1¼ pounds cooked shrimp

Directions
1. Add the oil to a cast-iron skillet and heat it over medium-high heat.
2. Add the garlic; stir-cook for about 1 minute until softened and fragrant.
3. Add the parsley, lemon juice, salt and pepper; stir-cook for a few seconds.
4. Add the shrimp and coat well.
5. Cool down and serve fresh or refrigerate and serve chilled.

Nutrition (per serving)
Calories 82, fat 3 g, carbs 2 g, protein 11 g, sodium 495 mg

Parmesan Brussels Sprouts

Serves 2 | Prep. time 5–10 minutes | Cooking time 10 minutes

Ingredients
2 cloves garlic, chopped
3 tablespoons butter, melted (divided)
6 Brussels sprouts, trimmed and halved
2 tablespoons shredded Parmesan cheese
Salt and ground black pepper to taste

Directions
1. Add 1 tablespoon of the butter to a cast-iron skillet and melt it over medium-high heat.
2. Add the garlic and stir-cook for about 30–40 seconds until softened and fragrant.
3. Melt another 1 tablespoon of the butter and add the Brussels sprouts, cut-side down; stir and cover the skillet.
4. Allow to cook for 4–5 minutes. Flip the sprouts and add the final 1 tablespoon of butter.
5. Cover again and cook for 2–3 more minutes until browned.
6. Serve with the Parmesan cheese on top. Season to taste with salt and pepper.

Nutrition (per serving)
Calories 203, fat 19 g, carbs 6 g, protein 4 g, sodium 291 mg

Garlic Potatoes

Serves 4–6 | Prep. time 5–10 minutes | Cooking time 25 minutes

Ingredients
1 large onion, thinly sliced
1 red bell pepper, diced
3 tablespoons vegetable oil
6 medium red-skinned potatoes, cut into bite-sized pieces
1 medium clove garlic, finely minced (optional)
1 teaspoon ground paprika
½–1 teaspoon salt
Ground black pepper to taste

Directions
1. Add the oil to a cast-iron skillet and heat it over medium heat.
2. Add the sliced onion and stir-cook until softened and translucent.
3. Add the garlic and bell pepper; stir-cook for 1 minute.
4. Add the diced potatoes, salt, pepper and paprika; stir and cover the skillet.
5. Allow to cook for 10–15 minutes until the potatoes turn soft and tender.
6. Uncover the skillet and increase heat to medium-high; cook for 8–10 more minutes until the potatoes are evenly brown, stirring occasionally.
7. Season to taste and serve warm.

Nutrition (per serving)
Calories 161, fat 7 g, carbs 22 g, protein 3 g, sodium 400 mg

Cranberry Asparagus Nuts

Serves 4 | Prep. time 5–10 minutes | Cooking time 15 minutes

Ingredients
⅓ cup pine nuts
⅓ cup dried cranberries
1 bunch asparagus, trimmed ends
3 tablespoons olive oil
1 pinch salt

Directions
1. Add the oil to a cast-iron skillet and heat it over medium-high heat.
2. Add the cranberries, nuts and salt and stir-cook for 5–6 minutes until the nuts become translucent.
3. Add the asparagus spears; stir-cook for 6–8 minutes until the spears are bright green and tender.
4. Transfer to a serving plate, spoon the nuts and cranberries on top, and serve warm.

Nutrition (per serving)
Calories 206, fat 16 g, carbs 14 g, protein 5 g, sodium 3 mg

Garlic Parmesan Green Beans

Serves 5 | Prep. time 5–10 minutes | Cooking time 10 minutes

Ingredients
1 medium head garlic, peeled and sliced
2 (14½-ounce) cans green beans, drained
1 tablespoon butter, melted
3 tablespoons olive oil
Salt and ground black pepper to taste
¼ cup Parmesan cheese, grated

Directions
1. Add the butter to a cast-iron skillet and melt it over medium-high heat.
2. Add the olive oil and garlic; stir-cook until softened and fragrant.
3. Add the green beans and season to taste with salt and pepper.
4. Stir-cook for 8–10 minutes until tender.
5. Serve warm topped with Parmesan cheese.

Nutrition (per serving)
Calories 157, fat 12 g, carbs 9 g, protein 4 g, sodium 555 mg

CHICKEN AND POULTRY

Lemon Asparagus Chicken

Serves 4 | Prep. time 10 minutes | Cooking time 10 minutes

Ingredients

¼ cup flour
1 pound skinless, boneless chicken breasts
½ teaspoon salt
Ground black pepper to taste
1–2 cups chopped asparagus
2 lemons, sliced
2 tablespoons butter, melted
1 teaspoon lemon pepper seasoning
2 tablespoons honey + 2 tablespoons butter (optional)
Parsley for topping (optional)

Directions

1. Cover the chicken breasts with plastic wrap. Pound to flatten to about ¾ inch thick.
2. In a mixing bowl, coat the chicken breasts with the flour, black pepper and salt.
3. Add the butter to a cast-iron skillet and melt it over medium-high heat.
4. Add the chicken breasts and stir-cook for 4–5 minutes per side until evenly brown.
5. Sprinkle the lemon pepper on top and set aside on a plate.
6. Add the asparagus to the same skillet and stir-cook until crisp and bright green. Set aside.

7. Arrange the lemon slices in the skillet. Cook without stirring to caramelize each side.
8. Serve the chicken with the cooked asparagus and lemon slices.

Nutrition (per serving)
Calories 232, fat 9 g, carbs 10 g, protein 27 g, sodium 344 mg

Shiitake Chicken Meal

Serves 4 | Prep. time 5–10 minutes | Cooking time 15 minutes

Ingredients
7 ounces shiitake mushrooms, sliced
4 (6-ounce) skinless, boneless chicken breast halves
Cooking spray as required
¼ teaspoon salt
¼ teaspoon ground black pepper
2 tablespoons butter
½ cup Marsala wine
2 green onions, finely chopped (divided)

Directions
1. Cover the chicken breasts with plastic wrap. Pound to flatten to about ½ inch thick.
2. Season the chicken breasts evenly with the salt and pepper.
3. Coat a cast-iron skillet with some cooking spray and heat it over medium-high heat.
4. Add the chicken breasts and evenly brown for 5–6 minutes per side.
5. Set aside the chicken and drippings; wipe the skillet.
6. Coat the skillet with some more cooking spray.
7. Add the mushrooms; stir-cook to tenderize for 2–3 minutes.
8. Add the wine and 3 tablespoons of the chopped onions; stir-cook for 30 seconds over high heat.
9. Reduce heat and add the butter; after it melts, add the chicken and drippings.
10. Serve warm with the remaining onions on top.

Nutrition (per serving)
Calories 291, fat 8 g, carbs 6 g, protein 41 g, sodium 303 mg

Chicken with Bacon and Apple Cider Sauce

Serves 4 | Prep. time 5–10 minutes |
Cooking time 15–20 minutes

Ingredients

4 (6-ounce) skinless, boneless chicken breast halves
¼ teaspoon ground black pepper
¼ teaspoon salt
2 bacon slices, chopped
½ cup fat-free, less-sodium chicken broth
¾ cup unsweetened apple cider
¼ cup minced onion

Directions

1. Cover the chicken breasts with plastic wrap. Pound to flatten to about ½ inch thick.
2. Season the chicken breasts evenly with the salt and pepper.
3. Cook the bacon in a skillet over medium heat until crisp. Set aside the bacon but leave the drippings in the skillet.
4. Add the chicken to the skillet and evenly brown for 5–6 minutes per side. Set aside the chicken but keep the drippings.
5. Add the onion and stir-cook for 2 minutes until softened and translucent.
6. Add the broth and apple cider. Bring to a boil and scrape the browned bits from the skillet.
7. Cook for 4–5 minutes until thickened.
8. Serve the chicken with the bacon and prepared sauce on top.

Nutrition (per serving)

Calories 269, fat 7 g, carbs 7 g, protein 41 g, sodium 412 mg

Pineapple Sweet and Sour Chicken

Serves 4 | Prep. time 5–10 minutes | Cooking time 12 minutes

Ingredients
1½ pounds skinless, boneless chicken thighs, cut into bite-sized pieces
2 tablespoons vegetable oil
1 small red bell pepper, cut into ¾-inch pieces
1 (8-ounce) can pineapple tidbits with juice, drained
¾ cup sweet-and-sour sauce

Directions
1. Add the oil to a cast-iron skillet and heat it over medium-high heat.
2. Add the chicken; stir-cook for 5–6 minutes until no longer pink.
3. Add the bell pepper and sauce; stir-cook for about 4 minutes until the pepper turns tender.
4. Add the pineapple and stir-cook for 1–2 minutes.
5. Serve warm.

Nutrition (per serving)
Calories 420, fat 15 g, carbs 34 g, protein 36 g, sodium 400 mg

Artichoke Pesto Chicken

Serves 4 | Prep. time 5–10 minutes | Cooking time 10 minutes

Ingredients
4 skinless, boneless chicken breast halves
Black pepper and salt to taste
2 teaspoons olive oil
1 (14-ounce) can artichoke hearts, quartered
1 (14½-ounce) can diced tomatoes (preferably with green peppers and onions)
¼ cup sun-dried tomato pesto

Directions
1. Season the chicken breasts with black pepper and salt.
2. Add the oil to a cast-iron skillet and heat it over medium-high heat.
3. Add the chicken; stir-cook until evenly brown. Set aside in a container.
4. Add the tomatoes to the skillet and stir-cook for 1 minute.
5. Mix in the artichokes and pesto; stir and add the chicken back.
6. Cover and simmer over low heat for about 5–10 minutes until the chicken Is cooked through.
7. Serve warm.

Nutrition (per serving)
Calories 228, fat 6 g, carbs 11 g, protein 30 g, sodium 866 mg

Classic Garlic Chicken

Serves 4 | Prep. time 5–10 minutes |
Cooking time 10–15 minutes

Ingredients

4 skinless, boneless chicken breast halves
3 tablespoons butter, melted
1 teaspoon seasoning salt
1 teaspoon onion powder
2 teaspoons garlic powder

Directions

1. Add the butter to a cast-iron skillet and heat it over medium-high heat.
2. Add the chicken, onion powder, seasoning salt and garlic powder; stir-cook until cooked through and juices run clear.
3. Serve warm.

Nutrition (per serving)

Calories 214, fat 10 g, carbs 2 g, protein 27 g, sodium 368 mg

Chicken Garlic Adobo

Serves 4 | Prep. time 5–10 minutes |
Cooking time 40–50 minutes

Ingredients
6 skinless bone-in chicken thighs
3 cloves garlic, minced
1 tablespoon vegetable oil
⅓ cup soy sauce
⅔ cup apple cider vinegar
1 teaspoon whole black peppercorns
1 bay leaf

Directions
1. Add the oil to a cast-iron skillet and heat it over medium-high heat.
2. Add the chicken; stir-cook for 5 minutes per side until evenly brown. Set aside in a container, reserving 1 tablespoon of drippings in the skillet.
3. Add the garlic to the skillet; stir-cook for about 1 minute until softened and fragrant.
4. Add the remaining ingredients and return the chicken; stir to combine well.
5. Cover and simmer the mixture over low heat for about 20 minutes.
6. Uncover the skillet, increase heat to medium-low, and cook for 15–20 minutes until the chicken is tender.
7. Remove the bay leaf; serve warm.

Nutrition (per serving)
Calories 251, fat 10 g, carbs 6 g, protein 34 g, sodium 1501 mg

Apricot Lemon Chicken

Serves 4 | Prep. time 5–10 minutes | Cooking time 15 minutes

Ingredients
4 (6-ounce) skinless, boneless chicken breast halves
Cooking spray as required
⅓ cup apricot spread
2 tablespoons lemon juice
2 tablespoons water
1 teaspoon curry powder
½ teaspoon salt
¼ teaspoon black pepper
2 teaspoons grated lemon rind

Directions
1. Combine the black pepper, curry powder and salt; rub the chicken with the spice mix.
2. Coat a cast-iron skillet with some cooking spray and heat it over medium-high heat.
3. Add the chicken; stir-cook for 5–6 minutes per side until evenly brown. Set aside in a container.
4. Add the lemon juice, apricot spread and water to the skillet; stir-cook for 1 minute.
5. Serve the chicken with the apricot juice and lemon rind on top.

Nutrition (per serving)
Calories 245, fat 2 g, carbs 14 g, protein 39 g, sodium 402 mg

Crumbed Honey Chicken

*Serves 4 | Prep. time 5–10 minutes |
Cooking time 10–12 minutes*

Ingredients

1 teaspoon + 2 tablespoons Dijon mustard (divided)
3 tablespoons honey
2 tablespoons butter, melted
4 (4-ounce) skinless, boneless chicken breast halves
1 cup dry breadcrumbs
Cooked broccoli florets or salad greens to serve (optional)

Directions

1. Cover the chicken breasts with plastic wrap. Pound to flatten to about ¼ inch thick.
2. Mix the breadcrumbs with 1 teaspoon mustard in a mixing bowl.
3. In another bowl, mix the remaining mustard and honey.
4. Coat the chicken with the honey mixture and then with the breadcrumbs.
5. Add the butter to a cast-iron skillet and heat it over medium-high heat.
6. Add the chicken breasts, stir-cook for 4–5 minutes per side until evenly brown and juices run clear.
7. Serve with cooked broccoli florets or salad greens on the side (optional).

Nutrition (per serving)

Calories 338, fat 9 g, carbs 34 g, protein 31 g, sodium 583 mg

Hoisin Glazed Chicken

Serves 4 | Prep. time 10–15 minutes | Cooking time 10 minutes

Ingredients
4 (4-ounce) skinless, boneless chicken breast halves
⅛ teaspoon ground black pepper
½ teaspoon salt
1 tablespoon vegetable oil
¼ cup low-sodium chicken broth
2 tablespoons hoisin sauce
1 tablespoon apricot preserves or fruit spread

Directions
1. Combine the apricot preserves, hoisin sauce and broth in a mixing bowl.
2. Cover the chicken breasts with plastic wrap. Pound to flatten to about ¼ inch thick.
3. Season the chicken breasts evenly with salt and pepper.
4. Add the oil to a cast-iron skillet and heat it over medium-high heat.
5. Add the chicken breasts; stir-cook for 3 minutes per side until evenly brown. Set aside in a container.
6. Add the broth mixture to the skillet and heat for about 3 seconds.
7. Add the chicken and stir-cook for 2–3 minutes; serve warm.

Nutrition (per serving)
Calories 186, fat 5 g, carbs 7 g, protein 26 g, sodium 526 mg

Butter Chicken Piccata

Serves 4 | Prep. time 5–10 minutes | Cooking time 15 minutes

Ingredients
4 (4-ounce) skinless, boneless chicken breast halves
¼ cup butter, cubed
¼ cup all-purpose flour
¼ cup white wine or chicken broth
½ teaspoon salt
½ teaspoon pepper
1 tablespoon lemon juice
Minced parsley (optional)

Directions
1. Combine the flour, pepper and salt in a mixing bowl.
2. Cover the chicken breasts with plastic wrap. Pound to flatten to about ½-inch thick.
3. Coat the chicken breasts with the flour mixture.
4. Add the butter to a cast-iron skillet and heat it over medium-high heat.
5. Add the chicken breasts; stir-cook for 5 minutes until evenly brown.
6. Add the wine and bring to a boil.
7. Cover and simmer over low heat for about 12–15 minutes until the chicken is no longer pinkish.
8. Sprinkle the lemon juice on top and serve topped with some parsley.

Nutrition (per serving)
Calories 265, fat 14 g, carbs 7 g, protein 24 g, sodium 442 mg

Pesto Bean Chicken

Serves 4 | Prep. time 5–10 minutes |
Cooking time 12–15 minutes

Ingredients

4 skin-on, boneless chicken thighs (about 1 pound)
1 cup red onion, finely chopped
1 Fresno pepper, thinly sliced
2 tablespoons olive oil (divided)
¾ teaspoon salt (divided)
¼ teaspoon ground black pepper
1 (15-ounce) can unsalted cannellini beans, undrained
⅓ cup prepared pesto of your choice

Directions

1. Season the chicken with the pepper and ¼ teaspoon of the salt.
2. Add 1 tablespoon of the oil to a cast-iron skillet and heat it over medium-high heat.
3. Add the chicken; stir-cook for 5–8 minutes until evenly brown and the skin is crispy. Set aside in a container.
4. Add the remaining oil, Fresno pepper and onion to the skillet; stir-cook for 1–2 minutes until the veggies are softened.
5. Add the beans and the remaining ½ teaspoon of salt; cook for about 1 minute.
6. Add the pesto and combine.
7. Serve the chicken with the bean mixture.

Nutrition (per serving)

Calories 423, fat 27 g, carbs 22 g, protein 23 g, sodium 615 mg

Chicken with Asparagus Bacon Bundles

Serves 4 | Prep. time 10 minutes | Cooking time 45 minutes

Ingredients:
4 x 4 ounce chicken breasts
12 asparagus spears, trimmed
4 slices bacon
½ cup water
Salt, black pepper
½ teaspoon paprika
¼ cup ghee
Extra virgin olive oil

Directions
1. Preheat oven to 375ºF.
2. Wrap each asparagus stalk with one slice of bacon.
3. Heat ghee in cast iron skillet over medium heat, add paprika.
4. Into ghee, place chicken breasts. Brown.
5. Place asparagus bacon bundles into skillet alongside chicken.
6. Place skillet into oven, and bake for 35 minutes.

Nutrition (per serving)
Calories 361, fat 14 g, carbs 4 g, protein 54 g, sodium 284 mg

Cornish Game Hen with Bacon and Onions

Serves 4 | Prep. time 15 minutes | Cooking time 30 minutes

Ingredients:
2 (1-1 ¼-pound) Cornish Game Hens
4 pieces of thick sliced bacon
24 pearl onions
1 teaspoon of salt
1 teaspoon of black pepper

Directions
1. Preheat the oven to 500°F.
2. Wrap a brick in aluminum foil so it is completely covered.
3. Place in the oven to heat thoroughly.
4. While the brick is heating, cut the game hen from the tailbone to the neck. Remove the backbone of the hen.
5. Next, fold the game hen open like a book and remove the keel bone.
6. Slice small slits into the skin just above the legs and tuck the drumsticks into the slits. This will keep your game hen from falling apart.
7. Repeat with the second game hen.
8. Season the game hens thoroughly with salt and pepper. Use as much or as little salt and pepper as you like. The recipe calls for 1 teaspoon of each, but you can use more if you like a saltier meat and less if you prefer the opposite.
9. Place a 12" cast iron skillet onto the stove, and set the temperature to medium.
10. Fry the bacon until it is crisp, usually about 5 minutes.

11. Reserve 1 tablespoon of fat from the bacon and remove the bacon. Set the bacon and reserved fat to the side, and drain the skillet.
12. Crumble the bacon.
13. Return the skillet to the stove.
14. Wash and peel the pearl onions. Place the whole onion into the skillet along with the tablespoon of drippings from the bacon.
15. Add the game hens to the pan, skin side up. You want the onions to be around the edges and not under the hen as you want the hens to be directly against the skillet.
16. Remove the brick from the oven, carefully, and place on top of the game hens. You may need to use 2 bricks depending on the size of your bricks.
17. Continue to cook on the stove for about 5 minutes.
18. Place the skillet, bricks and all, into the oven, and bake for 10 to 15 minutes. Use a meat thermometer and check the thigh meat. Once it reaches 170°F, the game hen is finished.
19. Remove from oven, and allow the bricks to cool slightly before removing them, about 5 minutes.
20. Serve the game hen warm, sprinkled with bacon and garnished with the cooked pearl onions

Nutrition (per serving)
Calories 206, fat 6 g, carbs 9 g, protein 26.7 g, sodium 238 mg

Chicken with Broccoli and Croutons

Serves 2 | Prep. time 15 minutes | Cooking time 20-30 minutes

Ingredients
2 large bone-in, skin-on chicken breasts
Salt and pepper, to taste
1 tablespoon vegetable oil or olive oil
1 large garlic clove, thinly sliced
1 small head broccoli, washed and broken into florets
1–2 large slices baguette or sourdough bread, torn into bite-size pieces

Directions
1. Preheat oven to 354°F.
2. Wipe chicken breasts dry with paper towels and season with salt and pepper.
3. Heat oil in skillet over medium heat.
4. Add the chicken skin-side down and let cook until skin is browned and crisp (about 4 minutes). Transfer to a plate and set aside.
5. Add garlic into skillet and sauté until fragrant (about 30 seconds).
6. Spread broccoli over skillet and place chicken, skin-side up, on top.
7. Let roast in oven until chicken is partially cooked (15 minutes).
8. Scatter the bread pieces over the mixture and continue roasting until bread is crisp and chicken is done (about 10–15 minutes).
9. Remove from oven and let rest for at least 5 minutes before serving.

Nutrition (per serving)
Calories 435, fat 21 g, carbs 19 g, protein 42 g, sodium 712 mg

Chicken with Spinach and Raspberry Stuffing

Serves 4 | Prep. time 25 minutes | Cooking time 25 minutes

Ingredients:
4 x 4 ounce chicken breasts
4 slices bacon
4 cups fresh spinach, chopped
½ cup frozen or fresh raspberries
½ cup cashews, chopped
Salt, black pepper
Coconut or olive oil

Directions
1. Preheat oven to 400ºF.
2. Create a slit in the side of each chicken breast, and slice in half about three-quarters of the way through.
3. Combine spinach, cashews, and a teaspoon salt and black pepper, along with 3 tablespoons coconut oil. Blend until combined but chunky.
4. Using a spoon, mix raspberries into the spinach mixture.
5. Spoon spinach into the slit part of chicken breast, wrap each breast in a slice of bacon.
6. Heat 4 tablespoons oil in cast iron skillet, carefully place each breast in skillet, and brown both sides.
7. Place cast iron skillet into oven and bake for 20 minutes.

Nutrition (per serving)
Calories 483, fat 14 g, carbs 15 g, protein 58 g, sodium 103 mg

Baked Asiago Chicken and Mushroom Pasta

Serves 4 | Prep. time 10 minutes | Cooking time 35 minutes

Ingredients:
4 chicken breast, skinless, boneless
½ cup Asiago cheese
8 Crimini mushrooms, stemmed
1 cup low-sodium chicken stock
¼ cup butter
2 teaspoons salt
1½ cup penne

Directions
1. Bring pot of salted water to boil, and cook pasta al dente.
2. Preheat oven to 350°F, quarter mushrooms, set aside.
3. Sprinkle chicken breasts with salt and slice against the grain into ½" wide strips.
4. Melt butter in a cast iron deep skillet, add chicken breast, brown.
5. Add mushroom, sauté for 2 minutes.
6. Add chicken stock, pasta, and sprinkle with Asiago cheese.
7. Cover skillet with aluminum foil, and bake in oven for 20 minutes.
8. Serve chicken with pasta.

Nutrition (per serving)
Calories 474, fat 33 g, carbs 15 g, protein 15.6 g, sodium 629 mg

Turkey Pot Pie

Serves 6 | Prep. time 20 minutes | Cooking time 55 minutes

Ingredients:
3 cups turkey, cooked and cubed
2 ½ cups cream of chicken soup (2 10.75-ounce cans)
1/2 cup of water
1/2 cup onion, chopped
2 cups mixed vegetables, canned (2 -15ounce cans)
1/4 teaspoon of salt
1/4 teaspoon of pepper
2 premade pie crusts

Directions
1. Preheat the oven to 375°F.
2. Take the premade pie crusts out of their tins. Place one in a 10" cast iron skillet. Set aside while you make the filling.
3. Place a saucepan on the stove, and set the temperature to medium-high.
4. Wash, peel, and chop the onion.
5. Mix together the turkey and onion in the saucepan.
6. Stir in the chicken soup.
7. Fold in the water.
8. Add the vegetables and stir thoroughly.
9. Stir the mixture occasionally until it comes to a boil, usually about 10 minutes.
10. Reduce heat and simmer for about 5 minutes.
11. Pour the mixture into the pie shell that is in the cast iron skillet.
12. Top with the second pie crust.

Nutrition (per serving)
Calories 488, fat 18 g, carbs 37 g, protein 20 g, sodium 629 mg

Cast Iron Turkey Burgers

Serves 4 | Prep. time 10 minutes | Cooking time 15 minutes

Ingredients:
1 pound ground turkey
1/2 cup yellow onion, chopped
1/2 cup apple sauce
1 garlic clove
2 tablespoons butter
1 tablespoon olive oil
1/2 teaspoon salt
1/2 teaspoon pepper
4 whole wheat English Muffins
Condiments for serving such as mayonnaise, ketchup, mustard, relish, sliced tomatoes, lettuce

Directions
1. Place the ground turkey and apple sauce in a bowl. Mix well. The apple sauce will keep the turkey burger moist.
2. Add the salt and pepper.
3. Place a cast iron skillet onto the stove, and pour in the oil. Set to a medium temperature, and heat the oil.
4. Mince the garlic, and place in the cast iron skillet.
5. Wash, peel, and chop the onion. Add to the cast iron skillet.
6. Sauté the onions and garlic until it is tender, about 3 to 5 minutes.
7. Add the onion and garlic mixture to the turkey, and mix thoroughly.
8. Shape into balls and press a whole in the middle.
9. Add a half to 1 teaspoon dollop of butter in the center.
10. Shape the turkey ball into a patty, but make sure the butter is in the middle.

11. Cook about 5 minutes per side, or until the meat is well cooked. Internal temperature must read at least 165°F on instant meat thermometer.
12. Split and grill the English muffins in the toaster. Add a patty and your favorite condiments on each burger.

Nutrition (per serving)
Calories 310, fat 111 g, carbs 23 g, protein 29 g, sodium 309 mg

PORK, BEEF, LAMB AND VEAL

Pineapple Pork Tenderloin

Serves 4 | Prep. time 5–10 minutes | Cooking time 30 minutes

Ingredients
Cooking spray as required
1 (1-pound) pork tenderloin, trimmed
½ teaspoon ground black pepper
2 tablespoons sugar
2 tablespoons dry sherry
¾ cup pineapple juice
1 tablespoon low-sodium soy sauce

Directions
1. Season the pork evenly with the pepper.
2. Coat a cast-iron skillet with some cooking spray and heat it over medium-high heat.
3. Add the pork; stir-cook for 3–4 minutes until evenly brown.
4. Cover and simmer over medium-low heat for about 10 minutes.
5. Turn the pork and simmer for another 10 minutes or until cooked through.
6. Slice into ¼-inch slices and set aside.
7. Combine the pineapple and other ingredients in a bowl.
8. Add the mixture to the skillet and boil until thickened and reduced to ¼ cup.
9. Pour the mixture over the pork and serve warm.

Nutrition (per serving)
Calories 191, fat 4 g, carbs 13.5 g, protein 23 g, sodium 243 mg

Sticky Orange Lamb Chops

Serves 2 | Prep. time 5–10 minutes | Cooking time 15 minutes

Ingredients
6 lamb chops, fat trimmed
7 ounces baby carrots
8 cloves garlic
3 oranges, zested and juiced
½ bunch fresh thyme

Directions
1. Season the lamb chops with sea salt and black pepper.
2. Arrange the lamb chops fat-side-down in a cast-iron skillet and heat it over medium-high heat.
3. Cook for 4–5 minutes until crisp.
4. Add the garlic and baby carrots; stir-cook for 2–3 more minutes until the lamb chops turn evenly golden.
5. Add the orange zest and thyme on top; toss well and set the lamb chops aside.
6. Add the orange juice to the skillet and cook until the mixture is sticky and bubbly.
7. Add the lamb chops and stir well.
8. Serve warm.

Nutrition (per serving)
Calories 517, fat 36 g, carbs 36 g, protein 26 g, sodium 312 mg

Mushroom Pork Chops

Serves 4 | Prep. time 5–10 minutes |
Cooking time 35–40 minutes

Ingredients
Garlic salt to taste
1 onion, chopped
4 pork chops
Black pepper and salt to taste
1 (10¾-ounce) can condensed cream of mushroom soup
½ pound fresh mushrooms, sliced

Directions
1. Season the pork chops with black pepper, salt and garlic salt.
2. Add the lamb chops to a cast-iron skillet and stir-cook over medium-high heat until evenly brown.
3. Add the onion and mushrooms; stir-cook for about 1 minute.
4. Add the mushroom soup and stir gently.
5. Cover and simmer over low heat for about 20–30 minutes until the chops are cooked to perfection.
6. Serve warm.

Nutrition (per serving)
Calories 210, fat 8 g, carbs 9 g, protein 23 g, sodium 924 mg

Spiced Lamb Patties

Serves 4 | Prep. time 5–10 minutes |
Cooking time 10–12 minutes

Ingredients

3 green onions, minced
4 cloves garlic, minced
1 pound ground lamb
1 tablespoon curry powder
Black pepper and salt to taste
¼ teaspoon red pepper flakes
Canola oil to cook
Salad greens to serve (optional)

Directions

1. In a mixing bowl, mix the garlic, curry powder, lamb, green onions, black pepper, cumin, red pepper and salt.
2. Prepare 4 patties from the mixture.
3. Add the oil to a cast-iron skillet and heat it over medium-high heat.
4. Add the patties; stir-cook for 5 minutes per side until evenly brown.
5. Serve warm with some salad greens (optional).

Nutrition (per serving)

Calories 237, fat 16 g, carbs 3 g, protein 20 g, sodium 140 mg

Peppered Sirloin Patties

Serves 4 | Prep. time 5–10 minutes | Cooking time 25 minutes

Ingredients
3 tablespoons all-purpose flour
4 (4-ounce) ground sirloin patties
Cooking spray as required
¼ teaspoon salt
¼ teaspoon black pepper
1 (16-ounce) pack bell pepper stir-fry
1 tablespoon low-sodium soy sauce
1 (14½-ounce) can diced tomatoes (preferably with balsamic vinegar, or olive oil)

Directions
1. Coat the patties with the flour and season with the salt and pepper.
2. Coat a cast-iron skillet with some cooking spray and heat it over medium-high heat.
3. Add the patties; stir-cook for 3–4 minutes per side until evenly brown.
4. Add the soy sauce, bell peppers and tomatoes; bring to a boil.
5. Simmer for about 15 minutes over low heat until the patties are cooked well and the veggies are tender.
6. Serve warm.

Nutrition (per serving)
Calories 246, fat 8 g, carbs 18 g, protein 25 g, sodium 785 mg

Mushroom Beef Stroganoff

Serves 4 | Prep. time 10 minutes | Cooking time 20 minutes

Ingredients
1 pound ground beef
1 (8-ounce) pack egg noodles, cooked and drained
1 (10¾-ounce) can condensed cream of mushroom soup
½ cup sour cream
1 tablespoon garlic powder
Salt and ground black pepper to taste

Directions
1. Add the ground beef to a cast-iron skillet and heat it over medium-high heat.
2. Stir-cook for 5–10 minutes until evenly brown. Drain excess fat.
3. Add the garlic powder and soup; simmer for about 8–10 minutes while stirring.
4. Transfer to a serving container and mix in the noodles.
5. Add the cream and season with salt and pepper to taste.
6. Combine and serve warm.

Nutrition (per serving)
Calories 679, fat 40 g, carbs 48 g, protein 28 g, sodium 660 mg

Potato Sausage Feast

Serves 6 | Prep. time 5–10 minutes | Cooking time 30 minutes

Ingredients
6 medium red potatoes, diced
1 pound smoked kielbasa, diced
1 red bell pepper, sliced
1 yellow bell pepper, sliced
1 tablespoon vegetable oil

Directions
1. Add the oil to a cast-iron skillet and heat it over medium-high heat.
2. Add the kielbasa and potatoes.
3. Cover the skillet and cook for about 20–25 minutes until the potatoes turn tender, stirring every 4–5 minutes.
4. Add the peppers and stir-cook for 4–5 minutes until tender.
5. Serve warm.

Nutrition (per serving)
Calories 404, fat 23 g, carbs 36 g, protein 13 g, sodium 697 mg

Spiced Squash Pork Chops

Serves 4 | Prep. time 5–10 minutes |
Cooking time 20–25 minutes

Ingredients
4 (4-ounce) boneless center-cut loin pork chops
½ teaspoon ground black pepper
¼ teaspoon salt (divided)
1 teaspoon pumpkin pie spice
1 butternut squash (about 1¼ pounds), peeled, seeded and coarsely chopped
1 cup onion, chopped
¼ cup water
Cooking spray as required
1 tablespoon fresh mint, chopped

Directions
1. Pierce the squash pieces with a fork; heat for about 1 minute in the microwave.
2. Season the pork evenly with the black pepper, spice and ⅛ teaspoon of the salt.
3. Coat a cast-iron skillet with some cooking spray and heat it over medium-high heat.
4. Add the pork and stir-cook for 3–4 minutes per side until evenly brown. Set aside in a container.
5. Coat the skillet with some more cooking spray, add the squash pieces and stir-cook for 6–7 minutes.
6. Add the onion and stir-cook for 5 minutes until softened and translucent.
7. Add the water and cook until the liquid is absorbed.
8. Season with the remaining ⅛ teaspoon salt and the chopped mint.
9. Serve the pork with the squash mixture on top.

Nutrition (per serving)
Calories 232, fat 7 g, carbs 18 g, protein 25 g, sodium 200 mg

Pork Chops with Swiss Chard and Fontina

Serves 2 | Prep. time 10 minutes | Cooking time 18 minutes

Ingredients
2 pork chops, about 1 inch thick
2 tablespoons olive oil, divided
Salt and pepper to taste
½ pound Swiss chard, stemmed, washed and cut into bite-size pieces
1 tablespoon grated Parmesan
¼ cup grated Fontina cheese

Directions
1. Preheat oven to 450°F.
2. Wipe pork chops dry with paper towels and rub with 1 tablespoon oil plus salt and pepper, to taste. Set aside.
3. In a bowl, toss the chard, salt and pepper to taste, and ½ tablespoon oil.
4. Spread over the bottom of a cast iron skillet.
5. Place the pork chops on top of the chard, at the center.
6. Drizzle the remaining oil over the chard and sprinkle with the cheeses.
7. Bake until chops are done (about 18–20 minutes, with internal temperature of 145–160°F).
8. Let rest for 3–5 minutes before serving.

Nutrition (per serving)
Calories 733, fat 60 g, carbs 5 g, protein 42 g, sodium 1061mg

Pork Loin with Sweet Potato

Serves 2 | Prep. time 15 minutes | Cooking time 55 minutes

Ingredients:
1 pound pork loin roast
1 sweet potato, peeled, sliced
1 red apple, cored, sliced
1 celery stalk, chopped
1 clove garlic, minced
1 teaspoon salt
1 teaspoon black pepper
Extra virgin olive oil

Directions
1. Preheat oven to 400ºF.
2. Heat 4 tablespoons extra virgin olive oil in skillet, place pork loin in skillet and brown.
3. Remove pork loin to plate.
4. Place sweet potato, apples, onions, celery, garlic on bottom of cast iron skillet, top with pork loin roast, and slide into oven for 45 minutes.

Nutrition (per serving)
Calories 431, fat 12 g, carbs 53 g, protein 27 g, sodium 107 mg

Seared Pork Chops

Serves 2 | Prep. time 10 minutes | Chilling time 12 hours |
Cooking time 35 minutes

Ingredients
1½ teaspoons sugar
1–2 tablespoons kosher salt
½ teaspoon black pepper
2 bone-in pork rib chops, 1½ inches thick
2 tablespoons vegetable oil
2 tablespoons butter
1 medium shallot, thinly sliced
8 sprigs fresh thyme

Directions
1. Combine the sugar, salt and pepper in a small bowl to make a dry brine.
2. Dry the pork with paper towels and season with the sugar-salt-pepper mixture. Place on a wire rack placed in a rimmed baking sheet. Refrigerate, uncovered, overnight.
3. After dry-brining overnight, preheat oven to 250°F.
4. Place everything (chops on rack, on baking sheet) in oven and bake until internal temperature is about 110°F (about 30–35 minutes). Remove from oven.
5. Heat oil in a cast iron skillet over high heat to smoking.
6. Add pork chops (reduce heat if there is too much smoke) and cook, flipping occasionally, until slightly browned (about 1–2 minutes).
7. Add butter, shallots, and thyme.

8. Spoon butter and shallots over pork chops (to baste and prevent shallots from getting charred), cooking until pork chops are golden brown. Using a pair of tongs, hold the chops sideways to brown the edges as well.
9. Transfer pork chops to a rack and let sit for 3–5 minutes.
10. Reheat the oil and drippings in the skillet to smoking and pour over pork chops.
11. Serve with vegetables or salad of choice.

Nutrition (per serving)
Calories 852, fat 62 g, carbs 1 g, protein 69 g, sodium 1008mg

Beef Corn Salsa Meal

Serves 4 | Prep. time 5–10 minutes | Cooking time 5 minutes

Ingredients
2 teaspoons chili powder

1½ cups frozen corn, thawed and drained

1 (16-ounce) jar thick and chunky salsa

1 pound ground beef

¾ cup cheddar cheese, shredded

Directions
1. Add the ground beef to a cast-iron skillet and stir-cook over medium-high heat for 7–8 minutes until evenly brown.
2. Add the chili powder; stir-cook for 1–2 minutes.
3. Add the corn and salsa and combine well.
4. Bring to a boil.
5. Cover and simmer over medium heat for about 4–5 minutes.
6. Add the cheese on top and allow to melt.
7. Serve warm with some cooked rice and/or tortilla chips (optional).

Nutrition (per serving)
Calories 374, fat 21 g, carbs 15 g, protein 31 g, sodium 1076mg

Mushroom Steak Tenderloin

Serves 4 | Prep. time 5–10 minutes | Cooking time 10 minutes

Ingredients

4 (4-ounce, ½-inch-thick) beef tenderloin steaks, trimmed

Butter-flavored cooking spray

¼ teaspoon salt

¼ teaspoon ground black pepper

1 cup baby Portobello mushrooms, sliced

2 tablespoons butter

1 cup dry red wine

1 teaspoon fresh rosemary, minced

Directions

1. Season the steaks with the salt and pepper.
2. Coat a cast-iron skillet with some cooking spray and heat it over medium-high heat.
3. Add the steaks and stir-cook for 3–4 minutes per side until evenly brown. Set aside in a container.
4. Coat the skillet with some more cooking spray, add the mushrooms, and stir-cook for 2–3 minutes to soften and brown.
5. Add the wine and cook until the liquid evaporates.
6. Pour the mixture over the steak.
7. Add the butter and rosemary to the skillet and cook until the butter melts.
8. Pour over the steak and serve warm.

Nutrition (per serving)

Calories 244, fat 13 g, carbs 4 g, protein 23 g, sodium 235 mg

Orange Ginger Beef on Egg Noodle Bed

Serves 4 | Prep. time 20 minutes | Cooking time 15 minutes

Ingredients:

16 ounces flank steak, thinly sliced
2 teaspoons fresh ginger, grated
½ cup fresh orange juice
¼ cup soy sauce
1 teaspoon salt, black pepper
Extra virgin olive oil

1 pkg (400-450g) egg noodles

Directions

1. Heat 3 tablespoons extra virgin olive oil in a cast iron deep skillet over medium-high heat. Add steak, brown for a minute.
2. Stir in remaining ingredients, and reduce heat to low. Cook for 10 minutes.
3. Cook egg noodles according to directions on package, drain.
4. Serve Orange Ginger Beef on Egg Noodle bed.

Nutrition (per serving)

Calories 457, fat 17 g, carbs 46 g, protein 27 g, sodium 100 mg

The Best Beef Sliders

Serves 5-6 | Prep. time 25 minutes | Cooking time 7 minutes

Ingredients:
2 pounds ground beef
2 large onions, thinly-sliced
1 tablespoon Worcestershire sauce
3 tablespoons flour
1 teaspoon salt, black pepper
16 buns
Extra virgin olive oil

Topping ingredients
Dill pickles

Directions
1. Combine ground beef, Worcestershire sauce, salt, black pepper, flour in bowl.
2. Divide beef evenly into 16 meatballs (approx. 1¾").
3. Heat 1 tablespoon oil in large cast iron skillet, add onions, and cook for a minute.
4. Sprinkle a little water into skillet to create steam.
5. Place approximately 6 slider balls on top of onion, and using spatula, press down to form patties.
6. Place bun halves on top of each slider, which will allow steam to cook through slider and warm bun at the same time.
7. Cook for approximately 5 minutes (do not turn over).
8. Serve topped with dill pickles.

Nutrition (per serving)
Calories 587, fat 30 g, carbs 40 g, protein 38 g, sodium 653 mg

Seared Buttered Steak with Red Wine Shallot Sauce

Serves 2 | Prep. time 15 minutes | Resting time 30 minutes | Cooking time 25 minutes

Ingredients

1 large bone-in T-bone (about 21 ounces and 2 inches thick)
Salt and pepper, to taste
¼ cup canola oil
5 tablespoons unsalted butter, divided
6 sprigs rosemary
2 large shallots, finely sliced
1 cup dry red wine

Directions

1. Wipe steak dry with paper towels and season well with salt and pepper. Let sit for 30 minutes at room temperature.
2. Heat oil in a 12-inch skillet over high heat.
3. When oil just begins to smoke, add steak.
4. Flip steak occasionally until edges begin to brown and crust (about 4 minutes).
5. Add 3 tablespoons of butter and rosemary.
6. Flip the steak to baste with the melted butter. Tilt the skillet to spoon butter and pour over pale spots of the steak. Reduce heat, if needed. Steak is done when internal temperature is at least 120°F (8 minutes). Cook about 1–2 minutes longer if medium or well-done steak is preferred.
7. Remove steaks from heat to a carving board, cover lightly with foil, and let rest for 10 minutes.

8. To make the shallot sauce, reduce heat to medium low, melt the butter in skillet, and add shallots until soft and fragrant, about 2-3 minutes. Increase heat to high, add wine, and bring to a boil. With a whisk or spoon, release brown bits of flavor from the bottom of the pan. Let the sauce reduce to desired consistency.
9. To serve, carve the meat, serve sauce on the side or drizzled on top of the steaks.

Nutrition (per serving)
Calories 885, fat 64.5 g, carbs 0 g, protein 72 g, sodium 782 mg

Roasted Steak and Potatoes

Serves 2 | Prep. time 10 minutes | Cooking time 45 minutes

Ingredients
8–10 ounces steak cut of choice, cut into bite-size pieces
1 large Yukon gold potato, washed, unpeeled, and cut into chunks
1 large red potato, washed, unpeeled, and cut into chunks
1 medium onion, sliced
2 tablespoons olive oil
Salt and pepper, to taste
1 teaspoon garlic powder

Directions
1. Preheat oven to 350°F.
2. Place steak, potatoes, and onion in cast iron skillet and drizzle with oil.
3. Toss to coat with the oil.
4. Sprinkle with salt, pepper, and garlic powder.
5. Bake until steak is browned and potatoes are tender and cooked through (about 40 minutes).

Nutrition (per serving)
Calories 577, fat 23 g, carbs 52 g, protein 40 g, sodium 708 mg

Garlic Lemon Lamb Chops

Serves 4 | Prep. time 5–10 minutes | Cooking time 10 minutes

Ingredients
3 tablespoons extra-virgin olive oil
3 tablespoons water
10 small cloves garlic, halved
2 tablespoons lemon juice
Ground black pepper and salt to taste
Pinch of dried thyme
8 ½-inch-thick lamb loin chops (about 2 pounds), trimmed
Pinch of crushed red pepper
2 tablespoons parsley, minced

Directions
1. Season the lamb chops with black pepper, thyme and salt.
2. Add the oil to a cast-iron skillet and heat it over medium-high heat.
3. Add the lamb chops and garlic; stir-cook for 3–4 minutes per side until evenly brown.
4. Set aside the lamb chops in a container. Keep the garlic in the skillet.
5. To the skillet, add the water, parsley, red pepper and lemon juice; stir-cook for 1 minute.
6. Serve the lamb chops with the lemon sauce on top.

Nutrition (per serving)
Calories 232, fat 18 g, carbs 6 g, protein 18 g, sodium 328 mg

Lamb and Butternut Squash Stew

Serves 4 | Prep. time 15 minutes | Cooking time 50 minutes

Ingredients:
1 butternut squash
12 ounces lamb
1 medium onion, sliced
3 cups water
3 tablespoons ghee
½ lemon, juiced
Salt and black pepper

Garnish
Parsley

Directions
1. Peel butternut squash, chop into 1" cubes, place aside.
2. Cut lamb into 1" cubes.
3. Heat ghee in cast iron pot, add lamb and brown.
4. Add onion, sauté.
5. Add butternut squash, lemon juice, water and salt, black pepper to taste.
6. Cover cast iron pot, and cook for 45 minutes or until squash is tender.

Nutrition (per serving)
Calories 244, fat 12.3 g, carbs 12 g, protein 22 g, sodium 279 mg

Lemon Caper Veal Fillets

Serves 4 | Prep. time 5–10 minutes | Cooking time 5 minutes

Ingredients
2 tablespoons unsalted butter
2 tablespoons capers
1⅓ pounds veal fillets
2 tablespoons lemon juice
1 tablespoon lemon zest
3 tablespoons basil, chopped

Directions
1. Remove the silver skin from the veal fillets; divide into 1-inch-thick medallions. Season with black pepper.
2. Add the oil to a cast-iron skillet and heat it over medium-high heat.
3. Add the medallions; stir-cook for 2 minutes per side until evenly rare.
4. Set aside on a plate and cover loosely with aluminum foil.
5. Add the butter to the skillet and melt it. Add the lemon juice, zest and capers; stir-cook for 1–2 minutes.
6. Serve the medallions with the lemon sauce and basil on top.

Nutrition (per serving)
Calories 230, fat 15 g, carbs 1 g, protein 21 g, sodium 213 mg

Veal Scaloppini Piccata

Serves 4 | Prep. time 5–10 minutes | Cooking time 10 minutes

Ingredients
6 tablespoons butter, melted (divided)
2 tablespoons olive oil
Flour to dredge
Salt and black pepper to taste
8 veal scaloppini
2 medium eggs (optional, for Veal Française)
1 cup chicken broth
Juice of 1 lemon
Fresh parsley and lemon slices to garnish (optional)

Directions
1. In a bowl, combine the flour, salt and pepper.
2. Coat the veal scaloppini with the flour one by one.
3. Add 2 tablespoons of the butter to a cast-iron skillet and heat it over medium-high heat.
4. Add half the scaloppini; stir-cook for 2 minutes per side until evenly cooked.
5. Set aside and repeat with the remaining scaloppini.
6. Empty the skillet, add the broth, and heat it until reduced to half.
7. Mix in the lemon juice and cook for 4–5 minutes until the mixture thickens.
8. Add the remaining butter and allow to melt.
9. Pour the mixture over the veal scaloppini and serve warm and garnish with parsley and lemon.

Variation: Veal Française

1. Beat the eggs in a mixing bowl. In another bowl, combine the flour, salt and pepper.
2. Coat the veal scaloppini with the flour one by one. Dip them in the egg mixture.
3. Cook in the skillet as above.

Nutrition (per serving)

Calories 218, fat 21 g, carbs 6 g, protein 5 g, sodium 309 mg

Veal Mushroom Marsala Dinner

Serves 4 | Prep. time 5–10 minutes |
Cooking time 10–15 minutes

Ingredients

1 cup all-purpose flour
2 tablespoons olive oil (divided)
1 pound veal medallions
Ground black pepper and salt to taste
1 pound fresh mushrooms, sliced
1 large shallot, minced
1 clove garlic, minced (optional)
1 cup dry Marsala
2 cups low-sodium chicken broth
1 cup low-sodium beef broth
2 tablespoons unsalted butter, melted

Directions

1. Season the veal medallions with salt and pepper; coat evenly with the flour.
2. Add 1 tablespoon of the oil to a cast-iron skillet and heat it over medium-high heat.
3. Add the medallions and stir-cook for 5 minutes until evenly rare. Set aside in a container.
4. To the skillet, add the remaining oil along with the shallots and mushrooms and stir-cook over medium-low heat until the veggies turn tender.
5. Increase heat to medium-high and add the Marsala and garlic; stir-cook until the mixture thickens.
6. Add both the broths; stir-cook until the liquid is reduced to ¼ cup.
7. Add the butter and allow to melt.
8. Serve the medallions with the mushroom mixture on top.

Nutrition (per serving)

Calories 491, fat 18 g, carbs 44 g, protein 23.5 g, sodium 314 mg

FISH AND SEAFOOD

Soy Glazed Cod Fillets

Serves 4 | Prep. time 5–10 minutes | Cooking time 10 minutes

Ingredients
2 tablespoons fresh ginger, peeled and finely grated
3 tablespoons rice vinegar
2 tablespoons soy sauce
4 (6–8 ounce) skinless cod fillets
Coarse salt and ground pepper to taste
6 scallions (green parts), cut into 3-inch lengths

Directions
1. Season the fish evenly with ground black pepper and salt.
2. Add the rice vinegar, soy sauce and ginger to a cast-iron skillet; heat it over medium-high heat.
3. Add the fish to the skillet and bring to a boil.
4. Cover and simmer over low heat for about 6–8 minutes until the fish is opaque.
5. Slice the chopped scallion greens lengthwise.
6. Add them to the skillet and combine well; stir-cook for about 2 minutes.
7. Serve warm.

Nutrition (per serving)
Calories 266, fat 2 g, carbs 14 g, protein 41 g, sodium 643 mg

Spiced Sweet Tilapia

Serves 4 | Prep. time 5–10 minutes | Cooking time 5 minutes

Ingredients
¼ cup low-sodium soy sauce
3 tablespoons light brown sugar
1 pound tilapia fillets
1 teaspoon Chinese five-spice powder (or your choice of spice mix)
1 tablespoon canola oil
3 scallions, thinly sliced

Directions
1. Season the fillets evenly with the spice mix.
2. Combine the sugar and soy sauce in a mixing bowl until the sugar dissolves.
3. Add the oil to a cast-iron skillet and heat it over medium-high heat.
4. Add the fish fillets and stir-cook for about 2–3 minutes until opaque.
5. Reduce heat to medium, flip the fillets and add the soy sauce mixture on top.
6. Bring to a boil, then simmer for about 2–3 minutes until the fish is easy to flake.
7. Add the scallions and combine.
8. Serve the fish warm with the gravy left in the skillet.

Nutrition (per serving)
Calories 180, fat 6 g, carbs 9 g, protein 24 g, sodium 596 mg

Classic Salmon Cakes

Serves 4 | Prep. time 10 minutes | Cooking time 10 minutes

Ingredients
1 small onion, diced
1 teaspoon ground black pepper
1 (14¾ ounce) can salmon, drained and flaked
2 eggs, beaten
3 tablespoons vegetable oil

Directions
1. In a mixing bowl, beat the eggs well. Add the salmon, onion and black pepper; combine well.
2. Prepare about 8 salmon patties from the mixture.
3. Add the oil to a cast-iron skillet and heat it over medium-high heat.
4. Add the patties and stir-cook for 4–5 minutes per side until evenly brown and crispy.
5. Serve warm.

Nutrition (per serving)
Calories 307, fat 20 g, carbs 2 g, protein 27 g, sodium 407 mg

Pepitas Lime Salmon

Serves 4 | Prep. time 5–10 minutes | Cooking time 6–10 minutes

Ingredients

½ teaspoon lime zest
2 tablespoons lime juice
2 tablespoons unsalted pepitas, toasted
1 tablespoon butter, melted
¼ teaspoon chili powder
4 (¼-pound) skinless salmon fillets
½ teaspoon salt
¼ teaspoon ground black pepper
Cooking spray as required

Directions

1. In a medium-large mixing bowl, combine the pepitas, lime juice, butter, lime zest and chili powder.
2. Season the salmon with salt and pepper.
3. Spray a cast-iron skillet with some cooking spray and heat it over medium-high heat.
4. Add the salmon and stir-cook for 2–4 minutes per side until evenly browned. Set aside in a container.
5. Add the pepita mixture to the skillet and cook until the butter melts.
6. Serve the salmon with the sauce on top.

Nutrition (per serving)

Calories 185, fat 9 g, carbs 1 g, protein 24 g, sodium 352 mg

Creamy Sautéed Scallops

Serves 4 | Prep. time 5–10 minutes | Cooking time 10 minutes

Ingredients
3 teaspoons butter (divided)
3 teaspoons extra-virgin olive oil (divided)
¼ cup low-fat sour cream
½ teaspoon salt
Ground black pepper to taste
2 large English cucumbers, seeded and sliced into ¼-inch pieces
1 tablespoon minced dill or flat-leaf parsley to garnish
1¼ pounds large dry sea scallops, tough muscle removed

Directions
1. Add the cucumber pieces to a colander and mix with some salt. Allow water to drain for 20–30 minutes.
2. Add 1 teaspoon of the butter and 2 teaspoons of the oil to a cast-iron skillet; heat it over medium-high heat.
3. Add the drained cucumber pieces and stir-cook for 2–4 minutes until brown and wilted.
4. Mix in the sour cream and stir-cook for 1 more minute. Set aside.
5. Heat the remaining oil and butter in the skillet over high heat.
6. Add the scallops, salt and pepper; stir-cook for 2–3 minutes per side until lightly browned.
7. Add the cucumber mix and stir again.
8. Serve with some parsley or dill on top.

Nutrition (per serving)
Calories 204, fat 9 g, carbs 12 g, protein 19 g, sodium 713 mg

Sausage Shrimp Jambalaya

Serves 4 | Prep. time 5–10 minutes |
Cooking time 15–20 minutes

Ingredients
1 (16-ounce) bag frozen bell peppers (preferably with onion mix)
1 (14-ounce) can reduced-sodium chicken broth
1 teaspoon canola oil
½ pound Andouille sausage, cut into ¼-inch-thick slices (you can also use low-fat kielbasa)
½ pound raw shrimp, peeled and deveined
2 cups instant brown rice

Directions
1. Add the oil to a cast-iron skillet and heat it over medium-high heat.
2. Add the bell pepper and sausage and stir-cook for about 3–5 minutes until softened.
3. Add the broth and bring to a boil.
4. Add the rice, cover the skillet, and cook for about 4–5 minutes.
5. Add the shrimp and stir.
6. Remove from heat and allow the shrimp to cook off the heat for 5–6 minutes.
7. Fluff the mixture and serve warm.

Nutrition (per serving)
Calories 392, fat 9 g, carbs 44 g, protein 27 g, sodium 650 mg

Wholesome Artichoke Spinach Salmon Meal

Serves 4 | Prep. time 5–10 minutes | Cooking time 15 minutes

Ingredients
4 salmon fillets
¼ teaspoon salt
1 tablespoon olive oil
¼ cup sun-dried tomatoes, chopped
3 cloves garlic, minced
6 ounces spinach leaves, chopped
1 cup artichoke hearts chopped
Salt to taste

Directions
1. Season the salmon fillets with the salt.
2. Add the olive oil to a cast-iron skillet and heat it over medium-high heat.
3. Add the salmon fillets, skins upwards, and sear for 3–4 minutes.
4. Reduce heat to medium; flip the salmon and sear for 4–5 minutes until flaky.
5. Remove the salmon and set aside.
6. Add the garlic, artichokes and tomatoes to the skillet; stir-cook for about 1 minute.
7. Add the spinach and stir-cook for 2–3 minutes until it wilts.
8. Add some salt, if desired.
9. Serve the salmon with veggies on top.

Nutrition (per serving)
Calories 278, fat 15 g, carbs 8 g, protein 25 g, sodium 547 mg

Mango Shrimp

Serves 4 | Prep. time 5–10 minutes | Cooking time 5 minutes

Ingredients

1 pound raw shrimp with tails, peeled and deveined
¼ teaspoon ground turmeric
¼ teaspoon salt
¼–½ teaspoon cayenne pepper
1 tablespoon extra-virgin olive oil
1 large ripe, firm mango, peeled and cut into bite-sized cubes
1 bunch scallions
¼ cup basil leaves, packed and finely chopped

Directions

1. Separate the green parts from the scallions, slice them, and discard the rest.
2. Toss the shrimp in a mixing bowl with some cayenne pepper, turmeric and salt. Cover and marinate in refrigerator for about 25–30 minutes.
3. Add the oil to a cast-iron skillet and heat it over medium-high heat.
4. Add the shrimp and stir-cook until tender and no longer pink on both sides.
5. Add the scallions, basil and mango cubes; stir-cook for 1–2 minutes until the scallions and shrimp cook through.
6. Serve warm.

Nutrition (per serving)

Calories 158, fat 5 g, carbs 12 g, protein 16 g, sodium 307 mg

Almond Crusted Tilapia

Serves 2 | Prep. time 5–10 minutes | Cooking time 6–8 minutes

Ingredients
2 tablespoons dry breadcrumbs
2 (6-ounce) tilapia fillets
¼ cup whole almonds
1 teaspoon garlic and herb seasoning blend, without salt
1 tablespoon canola oil
1 tablespoon Dijon mustard
⅛ teaspoon ground black pepper
Chopped fresh parsley (optional)

Directions
1. Add the breadcrumbs, almonds, seasoning blend and black pepper to a blender or food processor. Blend fine.
2. Coat the fillets one by one with the mustard and then coat evenly with the blended mixture.
3. Add the oil to a cast-iron skillet and heat it over medium-high heat.
4. Add the fillets and cook for 2–3 minutes per side until the fish is cooked well and easy to flake.
5. Top with the parsley (optional) and serve warm.

Nutrition (per serving)
Calories 367, fat 19 g, carbs 10 g, protein 39 g, sodium 321 mg

Simple Peppercorn Lemon Salmon

Serves 4 | Prep. time 5–10 minutes | Cooking time 8 minutes

Ingredients
4 (⅓-pound) skinless salmon fillets
¼ cup lemon juice
¼ teaspoon + a pinch salt (divided)
2 teaspoons canola oil
4 teaspoons unsalted butter
1 teaspoon green peppercorns in vinegar, rinsed and crushed

Directions
1. Season the salmon with the ¼ teaspoon of salt.
2. Add the oil to a cast-iron skillet and heat it over medium-high heat.
3. Add the salmon pieces and stir-cook for 5–7 minutes until opaque in the center.
4. Place on serving plates.
5. Combine all remaining ingredients in a mixing bowl along with the pinch of salt and pour over the cooked salmon.
6. Serve warm.

Nutrition (per serving)
Calories 226, fat 11 g, carbs 1 g, protein 28 g, sodium 269 mg

Halibut with Leeks and Carrots

Serves 2 | Prep. time 5 minutes | Cooking time 27-30 minutes

Ingredients
3 tablespoons extra-virgin olive oil
½ pound baby carrots
½ cup water, plus a little more if needed
3 medium leeks, sliced crosswise
Salt, to taste
White pepper, to taste
3 sprigs thyme
1 bay leaf
2 skinless halibut fillets, about 1 inch thick

Directions
1. Preheat the oven to 375°F.
2. Heat 2 tablespoons oil in a cast iron skillet over medium-high heat.
3. Stir-fry carrots until lightly golden (about 3 minutes).
4. Add water, cover, and continue cooking until carrots are crisp tender (about 3–5 minutes).
5. Add leeks (and a little more water, if needed), cover, and cook until soft (about 5 minutes).
6. Season with salt and pepper.
7. Add thyme and bay leaf.
8. Sprinkle salt and white pepper over fish and lay on top of vegetables.
9. Drizzle fish with remaining oil.
10. Top with parchment paper and cover with a tight-fitting lid.
11. Place in oven and bake until fish is cooked through (about 15 minutes).
12. Discards herbs and serve.

Nutrition (per serving)
Calories 457, fat 22 g, carbs 26 g, protein 42 g, sodium 157 mg

Wild Salmon with Fennel and Squash

Serves 4 | Prep. time 15 minutes | Cooking time 15 minutes

Ingredients:

4 x 4 ounce wild salmon fillets (1" thick)
2 medium yellow squash, sliced
2 fennel bulbs, sliced into strips
¼ cup slivered almonds
1 lemon, juiced and peel grated for 1 teaspoon of lemon zest
4 tablespoons olive oil, divided
Salt and black pepper
Olive oil oil

Directions

1. Heat 2 tablespoons of the olive oil in cast iron skillet over medium heat.
2. Add squash, fennel, and almonds, and sauté until veggies are tender. Remove to dish and toss with lemon juice, salt, and black pepper.
3. Add remaining oil into same cast iron skillet, and heat on medium.
4. Place salmon fillets skin-side up in heated skillet. Cook for 5 minutes, gently turn over, and cook for 4 minutes.
5. Serve salmon with veggies.

Nutrition (per serving)

Calories 438, fat 22 g, carbs 16 g, protein 46 g, sodium 168

Prosciutto-Wrapped Cod Filet and Zucchini

Serves 4 | Prep. time 10 minutes | Cooking time 20 minutes

Ingredients:
4 x 4 ounce cod filets
4 slices prosciutto ham
2 cups chicken stock
¼ cup sundried tomato, chopped
2 cloves garlic, grated
Salt and black pepper
Coconut oil

Directions
1. Preheat oven to 400ºF.
2. In bowl combine garlic, ½ teaspoon salt, ½ teaspoon black pepper and mix.
3. Wrap each cod fillet with a prosciutto slice.
4. Heat 4 tablespoons coconut oil in cast iron skillet, add cod filets to skillet and cook 3 minutes per side.
5. Add sundried tomato and garlic mixture to skillet, and place into the oven for 15 minutes.
6. Plate prosciutto-wrapped cod fillet with rice or zucchini noodles.

Nutrition (per serving)
Calories 300, fat 5 g, carbs 2 g, protein 59 g, sodium 611 mg

Pineapple Shrimp Stir Fry

Serves 4 | Prep. time 10 minutes | Cooking time 10 minutes

Ingredients:
1 pound shrimp, peeled and deveined
½ cup chopped pineapple
½ cup shallots, chopped
1 lemon, juiced
1 teaspoon salt
Extra virgin olive oil

Directions
1. Heat 3 tablespoons olive oil in medium cast iron skillet, add shallots, sauté for 2 minutes.
2. Add pineapple, sauté for 3-4 minutes or until a caramelization begins to take place.
3. Sprinkle in salt, add shrimp, sauté until pink, remove from heat.
4. Allow shrimp to sit in pineapple for a few minutes to soak in juices before serving.
5. Squeeze lemon juice over shrimp and serve with rice or noodles.

Nutrition (per serving)
Calories 300, fat 5 g, carbs 2 g, protein 59 g, sodium 611 mg

VEGETARIAN

Wholesome Spinach Zucchini Noodles

Serves 4 | Prep. time 5–10 minutes | Cooking time 10 minutes

Ingredients
2 cloves garlic, minced
2 cups spinach, chopped
3 medium zucchinis, unpeeled and spiralized
2 tablespoons butter, melted
¼ cup Parmesan cheese, grated
Salt and ground black pepper to taste

Directions
1. Add the butter to a cast-iron skillet and melt it over medium-high heat.
2. Add the garlic and stir-cook for about 1–2 minutes until softened and fragrant.
3. Add the spinach and zucchini noodles; toss well and stir-cook for 2–3 minutes until the spinach wilts. Do not overcook or it will get soggy.
4. Add the Parmesan cheese and toss to mix well. Season to taste with salt and pepper.
5. Serve warm.

Nutrition (per serving)
Calories 107, fat 8 g, carbs 5 g, protein 4 g, sodium 169 mg

Tomato Butter Beans

Serves 4 | Prep. time 5–10 minutes | Cooking time 5–10 minutes

Ingredients
2 (14-ounce) cans diced tomatoes, drained
1 tablespoon olive oil
2 cloves garlic, minced
1 (16-ounce) can butter beans, rinsed and drained
6 cups (about 6 ounces) baby spinach leaves
½ teaspoon Italian seasoning
¼ teaspoon pepper
Grated Parmesan cheese and cooked pasta to serve (optional)

Directions
1. Add the oil to a cast-iron skillet and heat it over medium-high heat.
2. Add the garlic and stir-cook for about 30–40 seconds until softened and fragrant.
3. Add the spinach, Italian seasoning, tomatoes, beans and black pepper; stir-cook until the spinach wilts.
4. Optionally serve with grated Parmesan cheese and/or cooked pasta. You can also refrigerate overnight and warm in the skillet when ready to serve.

Nutrition (per serving)
Calories 147, fat 4 g, carbs 28 g, protein 8 g, sodium 353 mg

Quinoa Peas Meal

Serves 6 | Prep. time 10 minutes | Cooking time 15–20 minutes

Ingredients
1 small onion, chopped
1 tablespoon olive oil
2 cups water
1 cup quinoa, rinsed
1½ cups frozen peas, thawed
¼ teaspoon pepper
½ teaspoon salt
2 tablespoons walnuts, chopped

Directions
1. Add the water to a cast-iron skillet and bring to a boil over high heat.
2. Reduce heat to medium-high, add the quinoa and stir.
3. Cover and simmer over low heat for about 12–15 minutes until the quinoa is tender and the water is absorbed.
4. Remove from heat and fluff the mixture. Empty the skillet.
5. Add the oil to the skillet and heat it over medium-high heat.
6. Add the onion and stir-cook until softened and translucent.
7. Add the peas; cook and stir until cooked well.
8. Mix in the quinoa and season to taste with salt and pepper. Sprinkle with the walnuts and serve.

Nutrition (per serving)
Calories 174, fat 6 g, carbs 26 g, protein 6 g, sodium 244 mg

Zucchini Noodles with Feta and Dill

Serves 2 | Prep. time 10–15 minutes |
Cooking time 5–10 minutes

Ingredients

4 medium sized zucchinis, unpeeled and spiralized
¼ teaspoon sea salt
2 tablespoons olive oil
1 clove garlic, minced
¼ teaspoon black pepper
½ cup feta cheese, crumbled
2 tablespoons dill, coarsely chopped

Directions

1. Add the oil to a cast-iron skillet and heat it over medium-high heat.
2. Add the garlic and stir-cook for about 30–40 seconds until softened and fragrant.
3. Add the spiralized zucchini; season with salt and pepper.
4. Stir-cook for 4–5 minutes until the zucchini is slightly wilted and softened.
5. Season to taste. Serve topped with the feta cheese and dill.

Nutrition (per serving)

Calories 334, fat 22.5 g, carbs 26.5 g,
protein 11 g, sodium 653 mg

Parmesan Sweet Potato Ribbons

Serves 4 | Prep. time 5–10 minutes | Cooking time 15 minutes

Ingredients
¼ cup sage leaves, stemmed
¼ cup Parmesan cheese, grated
2 medium sweet potatoes
2 tablespoons unsalted butter, melted
Ground black pepper and salt to taste

Directions
1. Peel the potatoes, cut into thick slices, and then shave to make ribbons.
2. Add the butter to a cast-iron skillet and melt it over medium-high heat.
3. Add the sage leaves and stir-cook for 4–5 minutes until crispy.
4. Add the potato ribbons and stir-cook for 4–5 minutes until tender.
5. Season to taste with salt and pepper. Serve topped with the Parmesan cheese.

Nutrition (per serving)
Calories 136, fat 7 g, carbs 14 g, protein 4 g, sodium 143 mg

Classic Skillet Corn

Serves 6 | Prep. time 5–10 minutes |
Cooking time 15–20 minutes

Ingredients

3 cups corn, cut fresh from cob
1 tablespoon sugar
¼ cup unsalted butter, melted
½ teaspoon salt
Ground black pepper to taste
½ cup water
1 tablespoon flour
¼ cup milk

Directions

1. Add the butter to a cast-iron skillet and melt it over medium-high heat.
2. Stir in the corn, water, salt, black pepper and sugar.
3. Cover and simmer over medium heat for about 15 minutes.
4. Combine the milk and flour in a bowl; add the mixture to the skillet and combine well.
5. Stir-cook for 4–5 minutes. Serve warm.

Nutrition (per serving)

Calories 158, fat 9 g, carbs 19 g, protein 3 g, sodium 267 mg

Cauliflower Flecked with Basil and Pine Nut

Serves 4 | Prep. time 10 minutes | Cooking time 10 minutes

Ingredients:
½ medium cauliflower
½ cup medium purple cauliflower
¼ cup pine nuts
¼ cup basil
½ lemon, juiced
1 teaspoon black pepper
1 teaspoon salt
2 tablespoons extra virgin olive oil

Directions
1. Slice cauliflower into small florets and salt.
2. Heat extra virgin olive oil, add cauliflower, and sauté for 5 minutes.
3. Add pine nuts, black pepper, continue to sauté for another minute.
4. Remove from heat, drizzle with lemon juice, sprinkle with basil, mix, and serve.

Nutrition (per serving)
Calories 215, fat 19 g, carbs 12 g, protein 5 g, sodium 626 mg

Garlic Asparagus Sauté

Serves 4 | Prep. time 10 minutes | Cooking time 30 minutes

Ingredients:
1 pound asparagus spears
1 red onion, sliced
2 cloves garlic
½ cup cashews, crushed
1 onion, juiced
1 teaspoon salt, black pepper
Extra virgin olive oil

Directions
1. Heat 4 tablespoons extra virgin olive oil in skillet.
2. Add onion and garlic, and sauté for a minute.
3. Add asparagus spears, cashew, salt, black pepper, and vegetable stock. Cover and cook on low for 25 minutes or until asparagus is tender.
4. Uncover and allow liquid to evaporate if still remaining.
5. Drizzle with lemon juice before serving.

Nutrition (per serving)
Calories 262, fat 22 g, carbs 15 g, protein 5 g, sodium 707 mg

Blistered Spanish Peppers

Serves 2 | Prep. time 1 minutes | Cooking time 3 minutes

Ingredients

1 tablespoon canola or vegetable oil

6 ounces Padrón peppers

Kosher or coarse sea salt, to taste

1 tablespoon extra-virgin olive oil

Directions

1. Choose a skillet wide enough to spread the peppers in a single layer.
2. Heat the oil in the skillet until it just begins to smoke.
3. Add the peppers in a single layer and let cook until they begin to blister (about 30 seconds).
4. Remove from heat, sprinkle with salt, and drizzle with olive oil.

Nutrition (per serving)

Calories 137, fat 14 g, carbs 2 g, protein 1 g, sodium 1140mg

Rosemary Sweet Potato Side

Serves 6 | Prep. time 10 minutes | Cooking time 35 minutes

Ingredients:
2 sweet potatoes, peeled
1 onion, sliced
1 red bell pepper, seeded, sliced
½ cup coconut milk
1 teaspoon rosemary
1 teaspoon salt
2 tablespoons extra virgin olive oil

Directions
1. Preheat oven to 375^{0}F.
2. Slice sweet potatoes into thin rounds (1/4").
3. Heat 2 tablespoons olive oil in cast iron deep skillet, add onions, sauté for a minute, remove pan from heat.
4. Place potato slices around the edges in a circle repeat circles inward, sprinkle with rosemary, salt, and add coconut milk.
5. Cover pan, place in oven for 30 minutes.
6. The Sweet Potato Side works great with any sort of meat or poultry dish or can accompany a tossed salad for a vegetarian meal.

Nutrition (per serving)
Calories 167, fat 4 g, carbs 32 g, protein 3 g, sodium 345 mg

Potato and Onion Flatbread

Serves 4 | Prep. time 15 minutes | Cooking time 20 minutes

Ingredients:
1 yellow onion
1 package of refrigerated pizza dough
1 russet potatoes
1 tablespoon of rosemary needles
1 teaspoon of salt
1/4 teaspoon of black pepper
2 tablespoons of olive oil
2 tablespoons of cornmeal

Directions
1. Preheat oven to 450°F.
2. Place a 12" cast iron skillet onto a stove, and set to medium heat.
3. Add the olive oil, and heat thoroughly.
4. Wash, peel, and slice the onions into thin rings.
5. Add to the oil, and cook until they begin to turn golden, about 5 to 7 minutes.
6. Place the onion in a bowl, and remove the skillet from the heat.
7. Wash and slice the potatoes into thin slices. Place in the bowl with the onions.
8. Spice with the salt, pepper and rosemary.
9. Toss the ingredients until the onions and potatoes are coated.
10. Either wipe out the cast iron skillet or use a new one of the same size. Turn it upside down.
11. Roll out the dough until it is roughly the same size as the bottom of the skillet.
12. Dust the bottom of the cast iron skillet with cornmeal.

13. Place the dough on top of the cornmeal.
14. Cover the dough with the potato mixture, making sure that you leave a 1" border around the edge.
15. Place in the oven, and bake until it is golden brown and the potatoes are soft.
16. Remove from oven and serve warm.

Nutrition (per serving)
Calories 276, fat 11 g, carbs 41 g, protein 6 g, sodium 1010mg

ZuCa Noodles

Serves 4 | Prep. time 10 minutes | Cooking time 0

Ingredients
3 zucchinis
1 carrot
½ teaspoon salt
3 tablespoons extra virgin olive oil

Directions
1. Peel zucchini and carrot.
2. Use a vegetable peeler, and peel zucchini until you reach seedy center. Save center for another recipe.
3. With the same vegetable peeler, peel carrot wisps.
4. Combine zucchini and carrots with 3 tablespoons extra light olive oil, ½ teaspoon salt.

Nutrition (per serving)
Calories 127, fat 11 g, carbs 7 g, protein 2 g, sodium 318 mg

DESSERTS

Lemon Poppy Seed Dump Cake

Serves 8 | Prep. time 5 minutes | Cooking time 30 minutes

Ingredients:
1 package lemon pudding mix
1 package Golden Cake mix
¼ cup poppy seeds
1 ½ cup milk
½ cup white chocolate chips
6 ounces butter, melted

Topping ingredients
3 tablespoons poppy seeds for topping

Directions
1. Preheat oven to 350^{0}F, lightly coat cast iron large skillet with a little butter.
2. In a bowl, combine lemon pudding mix, poppy seeds, Golden cake mix, milk, Golden Cake mix and butter, mix well
3. Pour batter into cast iron skillet, sprinkle with poppy seeds for topping.
4. Bake cake in oven for 30 minutes.

Nutrition (per serving)
Calories 243, fat 10 g, carbs 24 g, protein 3 g, sodium 268 mg

Cinnamon Raisin Nut Dump Cake

Serves 8 | Prep. time 5 minutes | Cooking time 20 minutes

Ingredients:
1 package Spice Cake mix
2 cups milk
½ cup raisins
¼ cup walnuts
½ teaspoon cinnamon
Butter

Directions
1. Preheat oven to 350⁰F and coat cast iron large skillet with a little butter.
2. Mix remaining ingredients in bowl, and pour into a large cast iron skillet. Place in oven for 20 minutes.

Nutrition (per serving)
Calories 157, fat 7 g, carbs 22 g, protein 4 g, sodium 108 mg

Maple Vanilla Custard

Serves 6 | Prep. time 10 minutes | Cooking time 10 minutes

Ingredients:
4 large eggs
4 cups milk
1 teaspoon pure vanilla extract
½ cup maple syrup
½ teaspoon salt

Directions
1. Whisk eggs in bowl, mix in vanilla, maple syrup, and salt.
2. Pour milk into cast iron pot, bring to simmer.
3. Remove milk from stove.
4. Add a tablespoon at a time of hot milk into egg mixture, mixing continuously in order not to cook egg.
5. Once egg mixture has been tempered with milk, whisk egg mixture into pot of milk.
6. Return pot to stove, and simmer for 5 minutes.
7. Cool and serve.

Nutrition (per serving)
Calories 250, fat 6 g, carbs 38 g, protein 11 g, sodium 147 mg

Raspberry White Chocolate Dump Cake

Serves 8 | Prep. time 5 minutes | Cooking time 35 minutes

Ingredients:
1 package raspberry pudding mix
1 package Angel Food Cake mix
1 ½ cup milk
½ cup white chocolate chips
6 ounces butter, melted

Directions
1. Preheat oven to 350^{0}F, lightly coat cast iron large skillet with a little butter.
2. In a bowl, combine milk, raspberry pudding mix, Angel Food Cake mix, and white chocolate chips.
3. Pour batter into cast iron skillet, drizzle with butter, and place in oven for 35 minutes.

Nutrition (per serving)
Calories 521, fat 15 g, carbs 58 g, protein 3 g, sodium 240 mg

RECIPE INDEX

ALSO BY LOUISE DAVIDSON

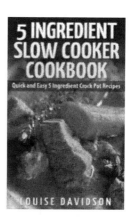

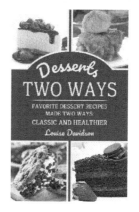

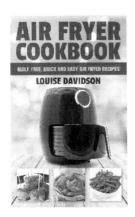

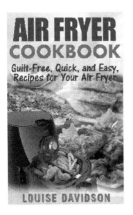
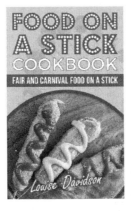
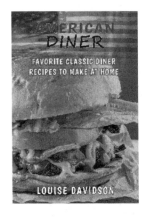

APPENDIX

Cooking Conversion Charts

1. Measuring Equivalent Chart

Type	Imperial	Imperial	Metric
Weight	1 dry ounce		28g
	1 pound	16 dry ounces	0.45 kg
Volume	1 teaspoon		5 ml
	1 dessert spoon	2 teaspoons	10 ml
	1 tablespoon	3 teaspoons	15 ml
	1 Australian tablespoon	4 teaspoons	20 ml
	1 fluid ounce	2 tablespoons	30 ml
	1 cup	16 tablespoons	240 ml
	1 cup	8 fluid ounces	240 ml
	1 pint	2 cups	470 ml
	1 quart	2 pints	0.95 l
	1 gallon	4 quarts	3.8 l
Length	1 inch		2.54 cm

* Numbers are rounded to the closest equivalent

2. Oven Temperature Equivalent Chart

Fahrenheit (°F)	Celsius (°C)	Gas Mark
220	100	
225	110	1/4
250	120	1/2
275	140	1
300	150	2
325	160	3
350	180	4
375	190	5
400	200	6
425	220	7
450	230	8
475	250	9
500	260	

* Celsius (°C) = T (°F)-32] * 5/9

** Fahrenheit (°F) = T (°C) * 9/5 + 32

*** Numbers are rounded to the closest equivalent

Made in the USA
Las Vegas, NV
21 February 2022